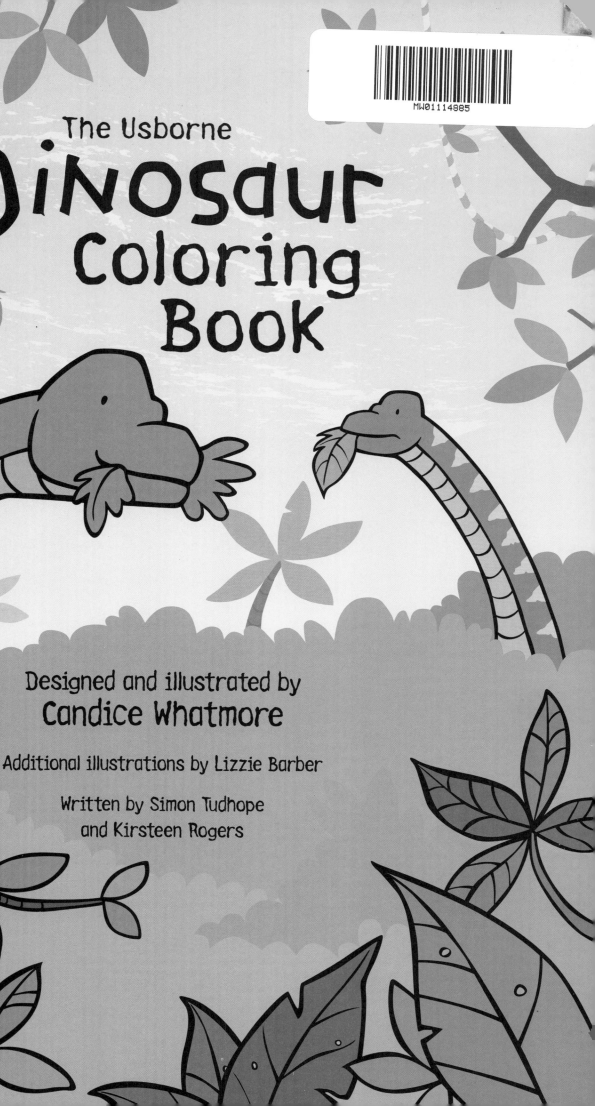

The Usborne
Dinosaur Coloring Book

Designed and illustrated by
Candice Whatmore

Additional illustrations by Lizzie Barber

Written by Simon Tudhope
and Kirsteen Rogers

Dimetrodon (dim-EAT-rod-on)

The big creature here is a Dimetrodon. It's not actually a dinosaur, although it looks like one. Its legs were on the side of its body, not underneath, so it walked with a waddle. Dimetrodons lived millions of years before the first dinosaurs.

How to draw a Dimetrodon

Use a pencil to draw a large oval.

Then draw a smaller oval.

Add a triangle.

Add a curved line.

Draw four legs.

Add a face, and a zigzag line to the "sail" on its back.

Use a pen to draw around the outline of the body.

Plateosaurus (plat-ee-o-SORE-us)

Plateosauruses were plant-eating dinosaurs. They roamed around in herds, looking for trees. When they found some, they stood on their back legs, stretched out their necks, and munched on leaves that smaller creatures couldn't reach.

How to draw a Plateosaurus

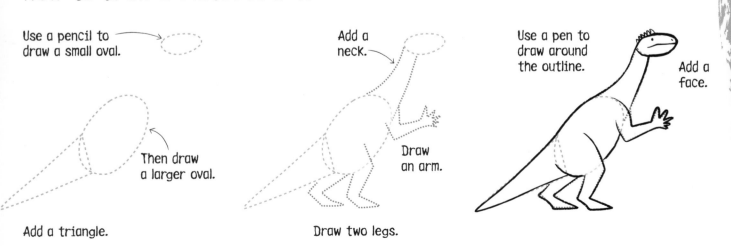

Use a pencil to draw a small oval.

Then draw a larger oval.

Add a triangle.

Add a neck.

Draw an arm.

Draw two legs.

Use a pen to draw around the outline.

Add a face.

Eoraptor (EE-oh-rap-ter)

Eoraptor was about the same size as a Labrador dog (but a lot less cuddly). It was light and fast, and ran after its prey on two legs. All the smaller animals were afraid of this nimble little dinosaur, with its large claws and nasty bite.

How to draw an Eoraptor

Use a pencil to draw half an oval.

Draw an oval.

Add a triangle.

Add a neck.

Draw two arms.

Draw two legs.

Use a pen to draw around the outline.

Draw a face and some sharp teeth.

Diplodocus (dih-PLOD-o-kus)

Diplodocus was a gigantic dinosaur. Its enormous neck allowed it to reach almost any leaf it liked, and it used its long, lashing tail to whip away its enemies. It may even have used its tail to help it swim across water.

How to draw a Diplodocus

Use a pencil to draw a large oval.

Then draw a smaller oval.

Add a long tail.

Add a long neck.

Draw four legs.

Use a pen to draw around the outline.

Add a face, and toes.

Stegosaurus (steg-o-SORE-us)

Stegosaurus had pointed plates on its back that stuck up like two rows of terrifying teeth. The bigger its plates, the more popular a male Stegosaurus was with females, because large plates showed what a strong, healthy dinosaur it was.

How to draw a Stegosaurus

Use a pencil to
draw a large oval.

Then draw
a small oval.

Add a
triangle.

Add two lines
for the neck.

Draw some big
pointed plates.

Draw four legs.

Use a pen to draw
around the outline.

Add a face and toes.

Archaeopteryx (ark-ee-OP-ter-ix)

Archaeopteryx was a bird about the size of a chicken, but unlike modern birds, it had teeth. Archaeopteryx couldn't fly very well and it probably used its feathery wings to glide from branch to branch.

How to draw an Archaeopteryx

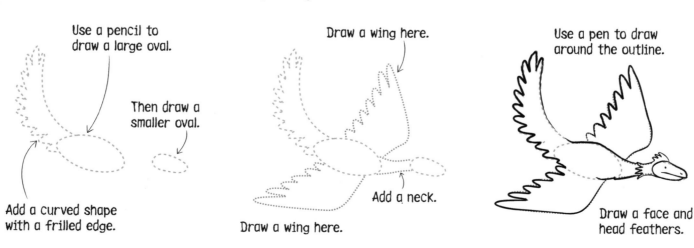

Use a pencil to draw a large oval.

Then draw a smaller oval.

Add a curved shape with a frilled edge.

Draw a wing here.

Draw a wing here.

Add a neck.

Use a pen to draw around the outline.

Draw a face and head feathers.

Plesiosaurus (plee-see-o-SORE-us)

Plesiosaurus was a huge sea creature that lived at the same time as the dinosaurs. It used its narrow flippers to paddle itself through the water, and darted its long, snake-like neck to and fro to catch fish in its tooth-filled jaws.

How to draw a Plesiosaurus

Use a pencil to draw a large oval.

Then draw a smaller oval.

Add a long neck.

Use a pen to draw around the outline.

Add a triangle.

Draw four flippers.

Add a face and teeth.

Ankylosaurus (ank-eye-lo-SORE-us)

Ankylosaurus was a plant-eating dinosaur. Its back was protected by a tough shield of bony plates, bumps and spikes embedded in its leathery skin. At the end of its tail was a bony club, which it probably swung at its enemies to defend itself.

How to draw an Ankylosaurus

Use a pencil to draw a large oval.

Then draw a smaller oval.

Add a curved tail.

Add a neck.

Add the tail club and back spikes.

Draw four legs.

Use a pen to draw around the outline.

Add a face and lots more spikes.

Tyrannosaurus rex (tih-ran-o-SORE-us rex)

Tyrannosaurus rex was a ferocious meat-eating dinosaur with a huge head, and powerful jaws for crushing its prey. Its legs were strong, so it could probably chase its victims quickly for short distances.

How to draw a Tyrannosaurus rex

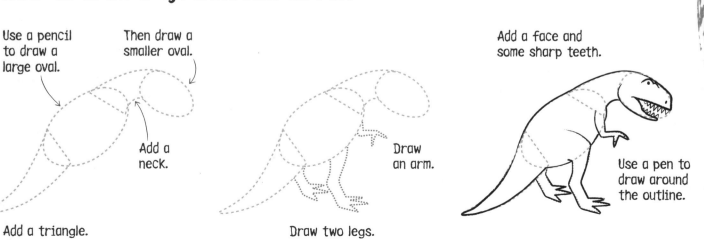

Use a pencil to draw a large oval.

Then draw a smaller oval.

Add a neck.

Add a triangle.

Draw an arm.

Draw two legs.

Add a face and some sharp teeth.

Use a pen to draw around the outline.

Pteranodon (teh-RAN-o-don)

Pteranodons were flying creatures that lived in prehistoric times. They used their leathery wings to glide through the air. They had no teeth, so when they caught a fish in their beak, they probably tipped back their head and swallowed it whole.

How to draw a Pteranodon

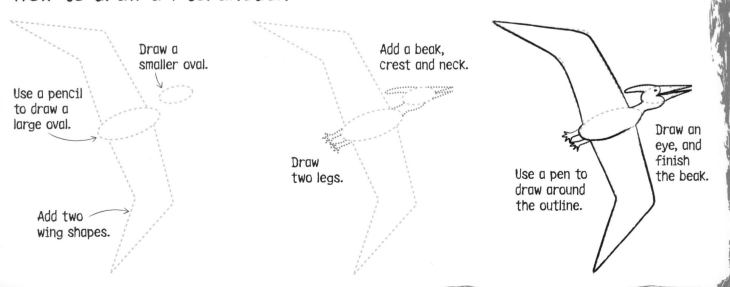

Draw a smaller oval.

Use a pencil to draw a large oval.

Add two wing shapes.

Draw two legs.

Add a beak, crest and neck.

Use a pen to draw around the outline.

Draw an eye, and finish the beak.

Triceratops (try-SERA-tops)

Triceratops was a plant-eating dinosaur. It was about the size of an elephant, and a large bony frill on its head made it look even bigger. Horns as long and thick as an adult's leg, and a sharp, parrot-like beak helped it fight off enemies.

How to draw a Triceratops

Use a pencil to draw a large oval.

Then draw a smaller oval.

Add a triangle.

Add a nose, three horns and a frill.

Draw four legs.

Use a pen to draw around the outline.

Add a face and toes.

Maiasaura (my-a-SORE-a)

Like all dinosaur mothers, Maiasaura females laid eggs with their babies inside. They dug holes in the ground to lay their eggs in, then watched over their newly hatched babies until they were strong enough to leave their nest.

How to draw a Maiasaura

Use a pencil to draw a large oval.

Then draw a smaller oval.

Add a curve along the back.

Add a snout.

Use a pen to draw around the outline.

Add a triangle.

Add a neck.

Draw four legs.

Draw a face.

Parasaurolophus (para-sore-OL-o-fuss)

Parasaurolophus had a tall, hollow crest on its head. Scientists think the dinosaur may have sucked in air through its nose and up into its crest, making a loud, deep noise. It may have sounded like a honking foghorn echoing around the forest.

How to draw a Parasaurolophus

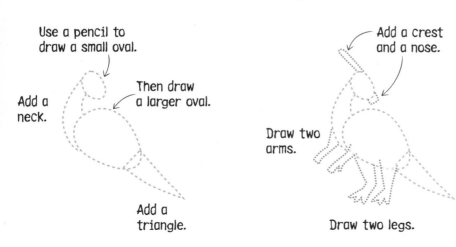

Use a pencil to draw a small oval.

Then draw a larger oval.

Add a neck.

Add a triangle.

Add a crest and a nose.

Draw two arms.

Draw two legs.

Use a pen to draw around the outline.

Draw a face.

Spinosaurus (spy-no-SORE-us)

Spinosaurus was probably the largest meat-eating dinosaur of all time. It was longer than a bus, and had a fin on its back as tall as a person. Its crocodile-like snout bristled with savage teeth, which it used to spear fish, and other dinosaurs.

How to draw a Spinosaurus

Use a pencil to draw a large oval.

Then draw a smaller oval.

Add a neck.

Add a curved hook for the tail.

Add the large fin.

Draw two arms.

Draw two legs.

Use a pen to draw around the outline.

Add a face and lots of teeth.

Dinosaur skeletons

Dinosaurs died out long before people existed, but their bones were buried in the ground, where they turned to stone. Scientists have pieced these together like giant jigsaw puzzles, to build skeletons that give us a clue to what different dinosaurs looked like. The dinosaur skeleton in this picture is a Stegosaurus.

How to draw a Stegosaurus skeleton

Use a pencil to draw a small oval.

Then draw a long back bone.

Add rib bones.

Add lots of pointed plates like these.

Draw four leg bones.

Use a pen to draw around the outline.

Add an eye hole, a mouth, and toe bones.

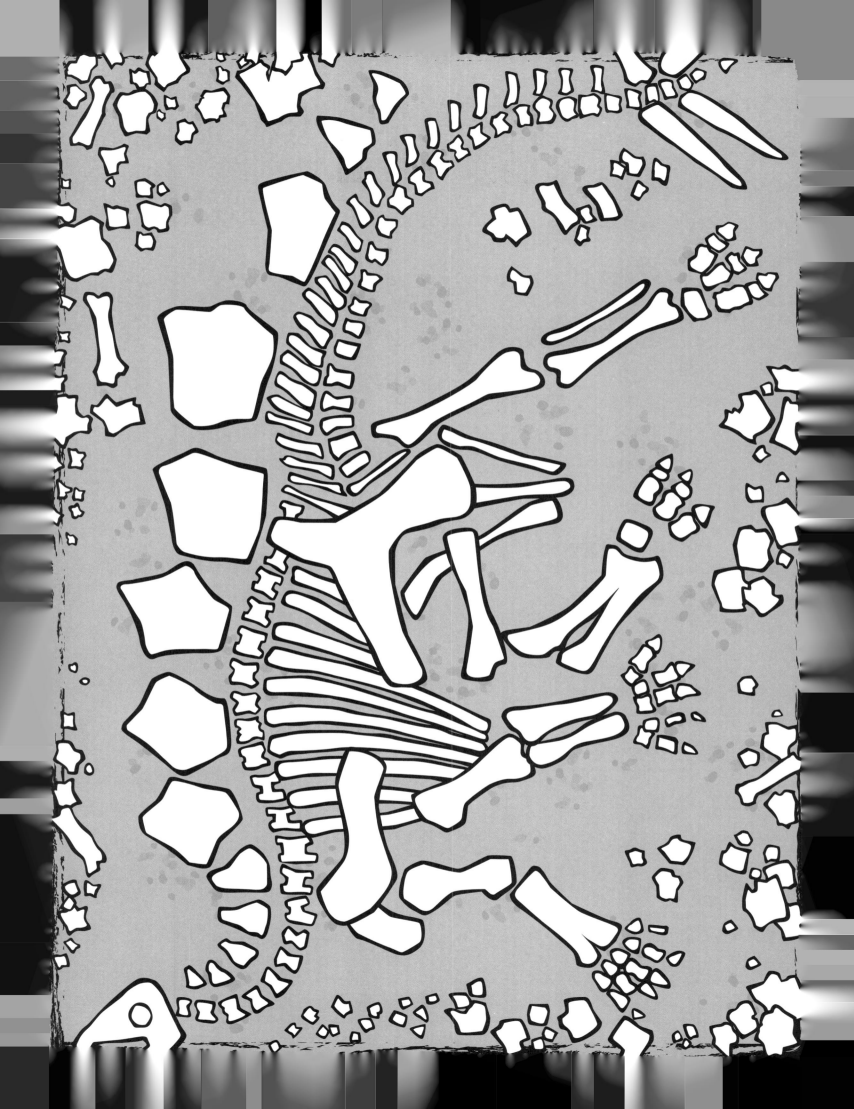

Coloring hints and tips

No one knows what color most dinosaurs were, so you can make them any color or pattern you like. Markers will give you strong colors, while pencils will have a softer effect.

You could finish this picture to practice coloring.

You can draw patterns within some of the shapes. For example, this scene is decorated with...

...zigzags and stripes...

...waves and wiggles...

...spots and dots.

Fill in larger areas such as this baby dinosaur with lots of lines going in the same direction.

It's a good idea to lay your book on a flat surface while you are coloring, or slip a piece of cardboard under the page you are filling in, to make a firm surface.

If you want to cut out your picture, you'll find a dotted line on each page to cut along.

With thanks to Keith Furnival. Dinosaur expert: Dr. Darren Naish
First published in 2010 by Usborne Publishing Ltd. 83–85 Saffron Hill, London ECIN 8RT, England. Copyright ©2010 Usborne Publishing Ltd.
The name Usborne and the devices ♈ 🌐 are Trade Marks of Usborne Publishing Ltd. All rights reserved. No part of this publication may
be reproduced, stored in a retrieval system, or transmitted in any form or by any means, electronic, mechanical, photocopying, recording
or otherwise, without the prior permission of the publisher. First published in the US in 2010. AE. Printed in Dongguan, Guangdong, China.